The Battle for the Sea

Ishani

Copyright © [2023]

Author: Ishani

Title: The Battle for the Sea

All rights reserved. No part of this book may be reproduced or transmitted in any form or by any means, electronic or mechanical, including photocopying, recording, or by any information storage and retrieval system, without permission in writing from the author.

ISBN:

TABLE OF CONTENTS

CHAPTER ONE

Aldous kneels beside a grave. His straight hair, more grey than brown these days, falls into his face as tears fall into the dirt below. His son sits across from him. His hair is the same as the dark brown patches still present on his father's head, but his is curly, loose coils that move along with his head. The grave is not fresh; a decade's worth of moss has grown to cover the headstone. Still, the holoprojector feebly shines on the mossy surface of the stone. The flickering inscription reads as follows:

Here lies Marta Fairley

Wife. Mother. Gone too soon.

1990 – 2025

With a sniff, the man straightens his back. His glasses have fogged with his warm tears, and the setting sun glints off of the wire frames.

"Righ' then," he says, as he stands and wipes the dirt from his trousers, "we should be leavin'. Sun's almost down, and we dinnae want tae be out past curfew." Aldous Fairley extends a hand to his son. "C'mon, Luca-lad. Time tae go home."

Luca takes his father's hand and rises. He already comes up to his father's chin, and Aldous is not a short man. The father puts his arm around his son's shoulders as they walk toward the cemetery entrance. They wind past headstones, shiny and new with metallic text next to crumbling edifices whose inscriptions have been matched by the surface after decades or centuries of wind and rain.

11

"Dad, how well do you remember Mum?" Luca turns his head to look into his father's face. Aldous looks straight ahead.

"I remember her like I remember ye, lad." He looks down and smiles at him. "As if she's standing righ' in front of me. 'Course, it helps tae have someone around who's her spitting image!" Aldous squeezes his son, and Luca laughs. His voice cracks a bit; he's getting to the age where that will only happen more frequently. For now, it only causes both men, young and older, to laugh even more, with Aldous adding tickling fingers to extend his son's laughter.

"Stop, stop! I yield!" Luca begs between wheezing laughs, his voice cracking once again.

"Oi, what's goin' on here?"

The laughter stops. Aldous and Luca stand up straight, both trying to catch their breaths rapidly. Two uniformed officers of the Imperial Police stand before them. One is tall, broad shouldered, and has his hat pulled low over his eyes. He carries a baton, which he rhythmically smacks into his left hand. The other is shorter, her longer hair wound into a tight bun low on her head. She holds a radio with a screen that glows ice blue.

"Sorry 'bout that, officers," Aldous says, shoving down his Scottish brogue as much as he could. "My son and I were just trying to lighten our moods after visiting his mother's grave. It's her, well, her anniversary, you see, and we were-"

"Young man, are you alright? Was this man hurting you?" The woman spoke then, her tone harsh and impatient.

"What? No!" Luca's eyes are open wide. Aldous can see the woman's radio, and can see a red light blinking. She's recording this. "He was tickling me! He was just trying to cheer us up!"

"Look, can ye tell me what this is all about?" Aldous' accent slips, and the taller officer catches it immediately.

"Are you Scottish, sir?" He turns toward Aldous, the cap still blocking the man's eyes from view. Aldous sighed and hung his head.

"Aye, Ah'm Scottish." He moves his right arm to show the white diagonal cross on the blue field emblazoned on his armband. "By birth. Ah'm a citizen of the Empire, though, have been since I was a lad, younger than him." Aldous puts his left arm around Luca's shoulder, and the officer stops smacking his hand with the baton.

"Sir, please unhand the boy and keep your hands where we can see 'em." Aldous does so, jumping back with his hands in the air. "What is your name, sir?" The man barks, and it takes every ounce of Aldous' fortitude not to make himself small.

"Aldous. Aldous Fairley."

"Aldous Fairley, eh? Teacher at the IA?" The woman speaks this time. Aldous nods in answer to her question. "We've heard of you. Some of the parents have expressed concerns that he, oh what was the wording?" She raises the radio and presses a few buttons below the screen. The man starts smacking his baton into his hand again, slower than before. "Ah, here it is! They're worried that he might, and I quote, 'instill dangerous values in our children by spreading lies about the Scottish Revolt.' Does that sound familiar, Aldous?"

"Wha-"

"Kid, if you don't shut your *bloody* mouth, I will *make* it bloody!" The man surges forward, baton poised to strike. Aldous jumps in the way.

"Dae not strike my son!"

"Aldous Fairley, Luca Fairley, you are under arrest." The woman's voice is cool and calm, almost smug.

"For wha'?" Aldous turns to look at her, eyes blazing with paternal fury.

"For being out past curfew." She looks around. The streetlights begin to turn on, one spotlighting Aldous and the male officer's altercation perfectly. Aldous just then noticed that the sun had set fully while he was in this situation.

"We're only out past curfew because *ye bastards* stopped us on our way home!" Aldous' patience is gone. His anger drains, though, as he looks at the woman. Dread settles in its place. She is smiling, a cruel grin, as she puts her radio into its place on her belt. The red recording light is no longer blinking.

"I think we have enough, don't you?" She looks at her partner. He looks back to her, a matching smile plastered on his face.

"Yeah, I think so." He turns back to Aldous and clicks a button on his baton. The end of it crackles with electricity. He changes stance, aiming for Aldous' gut.

"Luca, get away from here!"

"Dad, I'm not leaving-"

"Now!" Aldous pulls Luca out from behind him and pushes him toward the entrance of the cemetery. Luca stumbles, but he keeps going. The baton connects with Aldous' stomach and he cries out. The female officer tries to grab Luca's arm, but he evades her grasp. As Aldous sinks to his knees, he sees her give chase. The baton makes contact with the side of his head with a *crack*, and Aldous slumps to the ground. His glasses slip off of his face as he falls, one wire arm snapped under the impact of the baton. His vision is blurred, but he can still see the female officer run back. His ears ring too loudly to hear what they're saying, but he feels another jolt from the electrified baton tip pressing into his side. He screams and twitches, landing on his back. He feels a boot connect with his left ankle and hears a *snap*, feels another boot connect where the last jolt of electricity had hit, feels kicks all over, over and over. He tries to shield his face, but one boot comes down on his right wrist, crushing it and pinning it to the ground. He sees a boot raised over his face, and he closes his eyes, bracing for his last moment to be one of blinding pain.

But the pain does not come. His ears are still ringing, so he still cannot hear the words exchanged over his limp body, but he does not care. He slips into unconsciousness.

From a nearby alley, Luca watches the Imperial Police load his father into their car. He runs down the alley, not stopping when he feels his breath shorten. He runs through streets and alleys, nearly plowing into little old ladies on their way home from visiting with their neighbors. He runs and runs, his chest burning and his feet slapping the pavement. He does not stop until he makes it to a suburban neighborhood, brick homes nestled together with verdant gardens in front. He reaches a door, painted a deep blue, and knocks hurriedly.

"Auntie Mona! Auntie Mona, please help!" He knocks again, tears streaming down his face as he gulps down air. "Please, it's dad!"

The door opens, and a well-manicured hand takes hold of his arm and pulls him inside. Luca hugs the hand's owner, breathing in her perfume as he sobs. The floral scent calms him, and he stops crying after a few moments. The woman strokes his hair, detangling the nest of curls that had snarled as he ran. He pulls back, looking into her face. She is younger than his father, but a few streaks of grey have found their way into her hair as well. Hers falls in gentle waves, pulled back away from her face in a simple black barrette. Though Luca doesn't remember much about his mother, he sees a lot of her in his aunt, his mother's sister. Mona tucks a curl behind Luca's ear and looks into his eyes.

"Luca, you gave me quite a fright." She straightens her blouse, then puts a hand on Luca's shoulder. "What's happened, where's your dad?"

"They- they took 'im!" Tears threaten to fall again, but Luca screws up his nose to try and stop them from flowing. "They beat him up and put him into their car and drove away. They said we were out past curfew, but we only were because they stopped us leaving Mum's grave before the sunset. They woulda got me too, but Dad told me to run, and I did. I don't know where they took him, but I heard one of them say that he had to be alive." The tears overpower him now, and he buries his head in his hands, the heels of his palm pressing into his eyes to try and stop the flow.

"It's alright, Luca. It's going to be just fine. You did the right thing coming to me. I was just going to make some tea. Would you like some?"

Luca nods, forlorn.

"Right, sit down in the den, and we can talk about what to do next." Mona leads her nephew to the plush sofa and turns off the television, which had been showing some news show or another. She doesn't even remember now; all that's important is the boy in front of her. "I'll be right back, okay?"

Luca nods, and Mona ruffles his hair, undoing all of her careful detangling. Luca smiles, just a little bit, so she figures it was worth it. She steps into the kitchen and sets the kettle to boil. While she prepares two mugs with sugar and teabags, her phone buzzes from the counter. She picks it up as she hears the water start to move with the heat.

"Hey Mona, just checking in. Is everything alright?"

The message is from Jen Caldwel. She and Mona had lived together during Uni and stayed connected afterwards. Jen works with Aldous at the Academy, and also runs an advocacy group for prisoners transported off planet, trying to bring them home. Before Mona can respond, however, Jen sends another message. This one contains a link..

"Isn't this Aldous?"

Mona clicks the link, and it shows a news report. Aldous' picture, his official picture from the IA website, is at the top of the webpage. The headline reads, "Imperial Academy Robotics Teacher Arrested on Suspicion of Seditious Activity."

"Aldous, what the hell did you do?" Mona mutters as she skims the article, reading along with it.

It contains no information about his beating, or about him being out after curfew. It contains, instead, a glowing commendation of two Imperial Police Officers who arrested the "dangerous criminal" at great personal cost, as they both showed signs that the suspect had struggled against them. It even includes photos of the two officers, who sported bruising eyes and split lips.

Aldous had not, as far as Mona could remember, ever been violent with anyone. He was and is a kind soul, the man who stayed by her sister's side when she got sick, who took on single fatherhood and was the best parent he could be for Luca, who taught robotics to kids because he had always wanted to learn earlier, who had hope for the future. Mona, no matter how she might try, couldn't imagine him swatting a fly away, let alone hurting an armed officer of the law. She does the math, and it does not add up.

> **"Hey Jen. That is Aldous, but something feels off.**
>
> **Thanks for the heads up, tho!"**

She hears the whistling kettle and shakes her head, clearing the thoughts from it. Maybe Luca can help clear things up, once he's calmed down a bit. Her phone buzzes again with another message from Jen.

"Of course! Let me know if there's anything I can do.

Is Luca safe, do you know?"

"He's with me. We're just sitting down for a cuppa."

"Good! You both take care, then!"

"Will do."

Mona clicks her phone off. She takes the freshly poured tea into the den and sits next to her nephew. Luca takes his mug and wraps both of his hands around it, breathing in the slightly bitter smell of black tea, cut by the sugar his aunt had added. Mona hands him a spoon with which to stir his tea and offers him milk. He shakes his head, but stirs the tea. For a moment, the only sound in the whole house is the spoon clinking against the sides of the mug until, after three taps on the rim to shake off any drips, Luca sets the spoon down onto the spoon rest Mona had set in front of him.

Mona clears her throat.

"I know this is all still pretty raw, and it's alright if you don't want to talk about it right away, but I do have a few questions about what happened to your dad when you're ready to answer them."

Luca sips on his tea. Silence falls again as the streetlamps seem to burn a bit brighter. A car passes by, likely I-Pos trying to find anyone out after curfew. Luca still grips the tea mug in both hands.

"We were at the cemetery. Mum's anniversary. We were leaving, we were on our way home, the sun hadn't even set yet, and I asked Dad if he remembered Mum. He joked around a bit, and we were laughing. He was tickling me, and I'd just asked him to stop, when the I-Pos came 'round and asked if he was hurting me." Luca wipes a tear from the corner of his eye and holds his resolve. "I said no, and asked them to let us go. We hadn't done anything wrong. But Dad sounded funny, like he was trying not to sound Scottish, and his normal voice slipped back in when he got a bit annoyed at all the questions. Then, they started asking about his work, if he was talking about the Scottish Revolt or something like that."

Mona hangs her head. She'd heard from Jen that some of the parents were unenthusiastic about Aldous joining the faculty, but she hadn't known that they would go so far as to bring their unjustified concerns to the police!

"What happened next?" Mona lays a comforting hand on Luca's knee and looks him in the eye. Luca continues.

"One of them, a woman, said we were under arrest for breaking curfew, but we'd only been out as long as we were because of them! If they'd let us go earlier, or if they escorted us back since *they kept us out*, it would be *fine*! Dad would be *here*!" Luca is shouting now, the hurt and anger and fear he'd been bottling up spewing out like vinegar and baking soda. Hot, fresh tears fall into his neglected tea. "And then when I tried to say all that, the other officer, a man, looked like he was about to beat me, but Dad stepped in front of me and yelled at him. Dad made me run, but I didn't wanna leave him, so I hid when the lady I-Po ran after me. I still saw everything, though. They shocked him, and hit him, and kicked him." Luca stops, his throat raw from the sobbing account he gave. Once the words began, he found it impossible to stop. Mona rubs his back as he gasps for breath. "And then, then I ran here."

"Luca, did your father fight back at all?"

"No!" Luca whips his head towards Mona, curls bobbling in indignation. "No, he was just lying there! Most he tried to do was keep 'em from bashin' his face in!"

Luca does not often sound like his father, but it comes out most when he is upset. The idea that his father, a scholar who wouldn't even kill a spider that had bitten him, would fight with and hurt another person is absurd to him, and the fact that Mona suggested it in her "lawyer voice," that cool, even tone that she used when examining witnesses for the other side, makes him just upset enough for a little hint of Scottish to creep into his voice. Mona, for her part, holds her hands up.

"Easy, easy. I meant no harm by it." She takes out her phone and unlocks it, showing Luca the news story that she still had open. "I just wanted to make sure I knew how much shit the I-Pos were spewing with this." She lets him read the story, and she watches his face. He looks just as taken aback and aghast as she expected, and the hand that gives her phone back is shaking. "Listen: I believe you. I know your dad, and I know this isn't him. If his injuries are as severe as they sound, they've got him in a reconstruction pod right now, and he probably won't be back together, so to speak, for a couple of days. That means you can rest, get some sleep, and I can start putting together a strategy for his defense. I will fight this with everything that I can. Do you believe me?" Luca nods, the fatigue of fading adrenaline finally catching up to him. "Alright. Go on upstairs. I think I've got an old Uni shirt or something you can use as pajamas. When I see you in the morning, I should have a better idea of what we can do. And don't worry about getting up for school. I'll call first thing, tell them you're ill. You just sleep until you wake up. Alright?"

"Alright."

Luca's voice is smaller than Mona has heard it in years. He sounds more five than thirteen. He goes upstairs without another word, and Mona follows. She retrieves an old T-shirt from the bottom of a drawer and gives it to Luca, along with toothbrush, toothpaste, and a combo shampoo and conditioner that one of her ex boyfriends had left about a month ago. Luca shuts the door, and Mona heads back downstairs. She picks up her phone.

"Jen, here's the situation."

January 20th

No pain. This is the first thing that Aldous is aware of when he wakes up. There is no pain. He remembers being beaten, bones being broken, electricity sent through him twice, but there is no pain. He looks down at his left leg, expecting to see his foot hanging off the end of it, but he sees a perfectly healthy foot. He *sees*. Where are his glasses? He looks down at his right arm and flexes his wrist. Not broken. Fully functional. What is happening? A door opens.

"Ah, Mr. Fairley! Good to see that you're awake!"

A tall woman, so tall that he has to crane his neck up from the surface where he lies in order to glimpse her face. When he does, the remaining color drained from his already pale face. Her light blonde hair, sporting a single violet streak by her left temple, is immaculately styled for its short length. What little makeup she wears is in soft lavender and lilac hues that perfectly accentuate the similar undertones present in her skin. Her cloying smile is lacquered with a deep amethyst shade, and the teeth that show through are perfect pearls. Aldous has not met this woman before, but he has seen her photograph many times. She is Chief Constable Rezha Edwards, who oversees all Imperial Police activity for all of Northumberland.

"I was *so* disturbed to hear about your case. My officers were far out of line, particularly in their treatment of you and your son."

21

"My son? Is Luca-"

"He is alright, I assure you." Her voice is soft, with an allure to it that makes Aldous feel more at ease. He sits up from what he now realizes is a bed. "From what my *other* officers have told me, he ran to your sister-in-law and she has taken him in for the time being. I have demoted the officers who harassed you and treated you so savagely. I know that will not come close to repaying you for their actions, but I hope this may be of some further assistance." She hands Aldous a tablet, the screen displaying a letter. He takes it and reads. He sees something about a robot being built to automate factory output inspections on Fisian Moon 1, a desire to recreate and mass produce said robot in British and Fisian factories across the Solar system, and a request to send in a robotics expert as soon as possible.

"Ah'm sorry, my head still feels a bit…stuffed. Ah'm not sure what any of this has tae do with me."

"Well, as restitution for the libelous accusations of sedition, as well as a way to clear your slate with the parents who fund the Imperial Academy, I would like to recommend you for this studying expedition!"

"Wait, hang on, what 'libelous accusations'?"

"Ah, yes, of course! How could I forget. You *have* been under a proverbial rock for three days. Here, let me show you." Chief Constable Edwards takes the tablet back and taps the screen a few times, bringing up a news story. She hands the tablet back to Aldous. "This is what it looked like before I convinced my officers to retract their statements and tell the truth. The damage, I am afraid, has already been done." She quirks up a corner of her mouth, in an expression of sympathy. "The Parents' Council called for a hearing on the matter, and because you were not present to plead your own case, it was seen as a confirmation of your guilt. I hear your sister-in-law, along with one of your colleagues, fought valiantly on your behalf, but the vote still went against you."

Aldous stares at the screen, his brown eyes glistening with unshed tears.

"But, one could imagine that such a sacrifice for monarch, advisors, and Empire would change the tide to your favor. A quick flight out to Fisian Moon 1, a day or two of studying this machine, and another quick flight back home would make you a hero of the Empire, and what of these parents would not want their offspring instructed by such a hero, regardless of their prior hesitations based on nothing but his country of origin?" She leans down to Aldous' level, catching his brown eyes with her own violet ones. "After all, instructors and authorities with much more, well, *alien* backgrounds do not seem to bother them at all, simply because your monarch has endorsed us."

"I appreciate the sentiment, Chief Constable, I really do. However, Ah cannae justify leaving my son behind. What ye've called a 'quick flight' only feels that way because of the Cryo. This will take a *minimum* of ten years, not even factoring in the time needed for study. If anything proves too complex, or if we run intae any pushback from the machine's creator, it will be longer. I cannae leave my son now and come back when he's a grown man."

The sympathetic twinge of the Chief Constable's lips disappears and is replaced by a thin purple line. She closes her eyes and draws herself up to her full height. She walks back to the door, which she had left ajar when she entered. She closes it now, silently, and stalks back toward Aldous.

"Perhaps I did not make myself quite clear." The softness remains in her voice, but there is a decided sharpness to it as well. Her eyes narrow and she looms over Aldous. "This is the *only* way to improve your standing with the Parents' Council. Are you no longer interested in teaching at the Academy?"

"If it's a choice between teaching at the Academy, or anywhere else, and staying with my son, then I would gladly retire early or find some other career."

"And if you have no choice?" The kindness is completely gone now. The violet eyes flash with indignation and she grabs Aldous by the front of the garment he's wearing, bringing him up to eye level with her. He lifts about half a foot off of the ground. "If my 'offer' was a command? Would you attempt to defy the orders of your monarch?"

Aldous' mouth goes dry. In that moment, as his toes just barely scrape the ground, he understands.

"Those officers kept me out past curfew intentionally, didn't they? They knew who I was. They were sent to find me and bring me in."

"Very good! You *are* as clever as your file suggests!" Chief Constable Edwards sets Aldous down on his feet again. "So now you can see how pointless it is to attempt to evade this appointment of yours." She turns away from him, strolling around the room in order to illustrate again just how much taller she is. "If you run, the police force will be looking for you. If you hide, we *will* find you. If we must, we will even find your son, Luca, was it? We will find him and hold him until you comply. Kids his age get up to all sorts of things, after all. It would not be difficult to ensure that he falls into unsavory company and commits some infringing act that would require our intervention."

"Leave him out of this." Aldous' hands balled into fists at his sides.

"You are the one who brought him into this, Mr. Fairley!"

She looks back at him, slowly, languidly. None of this bothers her. She is as placid as a man-made pool, unperturbed by natural waves of emotion. Her expression is detached, betraying that her thoughts are not fully here in the moment. She is already planning contingencies for the million scenarios in which she must capture, injure, maim, or kill Luca Fairley if his father does not comply with her order.

"You set him up as the one obstacle to your accepting this position, so you forced me to think of ways to eliminate the obstacle. Now, are you going to comply, or will I have to involve your son further?"

Aldous stares at his feet, thoughts racing through his head before he can catch them whole. *I promised Marta- I cannae let them- I cannae leave- Where will he- How will I-* The thoughts run their course within the blink of an eye, and a winner steps forward into clarity.

"Will I still be able tae communicate with 'im?"

"Of course, Mr. Fairley!" The warmth returns to Edwards' voice. "You're not being *transported*, after all. The accusations of sedition were proven false. You've been appointed for a specialized mission." She kneels, allowing her to look into Aldous' downcast eyes. "You have been asked to serve Emperor William the Fifth of Unified Britannia, as well as Emperor Yiiv-Taal of Fisia-Hu'Tu, in a very minor endeavor."

"And there's no one else who can dae this?"

"Unfortunately, no. There are very few Fisian technicians, as many of them choose to serve in the political realm, and the one who oversaw the factory where the machine you will study was implemented is the reason one of the Hu'Tu workers created the machine in the first place, so we cannot expect an objective report from them. We need someone who has never seen the machine before, so that they can make the most objective observations possible."

"Aright," Aldous says, defeat lacing his words. "Ah'll take the assignment. How long do I have to get my things in order, sort out Luca, all of that?"

"The transport will leave whenever you are ready, but I would recommend you make things as 'speedy' as possible. I will check in with you personally if you are not ready within a month."

"That shouldnae be needed, thanks. But a week would be fine?"

"Of course. Though, if you would like to leave earlier for whatever reason, please do not hesitate to let me know. Transport can be arranged at a moment's notice."

"Of course." Aldous looks Chief Constable Edwards in the eye. "Am I free to leave?"

"Yes, by all means!" She strides to the door, opening it with a fluid twist of her wrist. "Is there anyone you would like to call to pick you up, or somewhere my officers can escort you?"

"I'd like to call my sister-in-law. You said she had Luca?"

"That is correct. Your belongings should be waiting for you at the receptionists' desk out front. Your cell phone should be with the rest of your things."

Chief Constable Edwards gestures for Aldous to walk through the door. He hesitates, wondering if it is some kind of trap or a genuine opportunity to leave. He takes a step towards the open door, then another. Once he reaches the door, the Chief Constable puts a heavy hand on his shoulder. She leans down close to his ear.

"Remember, Mr. Fairley: you have agreed to this, and failure to comply will have repercussions on your son."

Aldous nods, swallowing down his urge to scream in her face. He just needs to leave, to see Luca, to make the most of the week he bought for himself. Giving in and resisting, fighting back against this, would only make things worse. He could be shipped off within an hour, issued necessaries for the trip and stuck in a Cryo pod. She notes the tenuous hold he has on his emotions and smirks.

"Your Emperor thanks you for your service, Aldous."

Aldous rushes out of the station, stopping in the lobby only long enough to pick up what he had been carrying when he was brought in here. His cell is hanging on by a thread of charge, not enough for a phone call, so he uses that thread to send a text to Mona.

"I'm alright, just leaving the police station.

Could you or a colleague come to get me?"

As he sees that the message was delivered, the phone dies in his hand. Powerless to do anything but to wait for a retrieval, Aldous sits on the curb outside of the police station and weeps.

Mona receives Aldous' text while helping Luca with his homework. Imperial History, unfortunately her best subject. When she reads the text from Aldous, her eyes light up just enough for Luca to notice.

"Everything alright?"

"Better! Your dad's just been released. We can go pick him up from the police station."

Luca shoots up from his seat at Mona's kitchen table with enough force to knock the chair over. As it clatters to the ground, Luca races to hug his aunt. Mona squeezes him tight, truly breathing easy for the first time since he ran to her door. He feels one arm move, likely to reply to the text, and he takes that as his cue to run and put on his shoes. He slides on the polished wood floor of Mona's entryway and sits on the ground to pull on his sneakers.

Mona takes her handbag from the hook by the garage door and checks to make sure her keys are inside. Luca bolts to her side, all boyish energy and wide grin. He bounces on the balls of his feet, impatient to leave and to see his father again, to make sure he is safe and well and coming home. Mona locates her keys and goes to her car, watching Luca clamber into the passenger seat.

They do not speak on the way, Luca from sheer excitement and Mona from deep pondering. She wonders why they let him leave, if they had *finally* realized that he was no threat to the Empire, if there was a condition to his release. None of these questions, which she had asked in her reply to Aldous' message, had received an answer yet. No doubt his phone battery had died, given that the I-Pos probably hadn't thought to charge it. The silence lasts until Luca could see his father on the curb, head buried in his hands.

"Look! There he is! He looks... he looks upset."

Mona had to agree with her nephew's assessment. That does not look like a man who's just been exonerated. That looks like a man who has lost all of his hope.

Before Mona can fully stop the vehicle, Luca is out of it and running to his dad. The boy shouts, and Aldous raises his head. He throws out his arms, and Luca falls into them. Mona parks the car and joins them. She keeps back a bit, though. She doesn't want to spoil the moment. Aldous is crying again, but they are tears of joy this time.

"Are you alright? Did they hurt you again? Why were you crying?" The questions fly out of Luca's mouth at breakneck speeds. Aldous laughs, after a sniffle, and ruffles the boy's hair.

"I'm fine, they dinnae hurt me. An' I was crying because... well, Ah cannae really say righ' now. Ah'll tell you as soon as we get home, so let's go on, aright? Help me up, will ye?" Luca jumps up and extends his hand to his father. With a grunt and a struggle, Aldous rises from the curb. He looks over to Mona now, finally seeing her. "Thanks for taking him on, Mona."

"Of course! I've loved having him. He's been a perfect houseguest. You've done well, raising him. I think Marta would be proud."

"Thank ye."

Tears close up Aldous' throat again. He hugs his son even tighter. In silence, they all climb into the car. Luca sits in the backseat, leaving the passenger seat open for Aldous, but the father chooses to sit in the back as well. Without saying why, Aldous spends the ride to his and Luca's home holding his son's hand as tight as he can.

Mona catches glimpses of his face in the rear-view mirror, and the face she sees is that of a broken man. The broken bones had healed, likely thanks to a reconstruction pod, but his spirit is fractured. He tries to hide it, looking out the window so that Luca cannot see his face, but Aldous has lost a bit of his optimism, a bit of his softness. Mona barely recognizes this attitude in him, but she *has* seen it before. She has seen it in the eyes of clients who were transported for their crimes, ripped away from everything and everyone they knew. Is this why he had been crying when they pulled up?

When they arrive at Aldous and Luca's home, a flat in Academy faculty housing, Mona sees a familiar woman. Jen Caldwel. She had just been in to see another friend, a colleague whose wife had just given birth, and to bring them a meal. She carries an empty casserole carrier, holding it in one hand while she pulls her straight blonde hair out from under her scarf. Mona parks her car and goes to talk to Jen, hoping to give Aldous and Luca some time to themselves.

"Mona! Is that Aldous, is he alright?" Mona nods, watching Aldous and Luca walk inside.

Jen's face is full of the most genuine concern that Mona has ever seen. When they first met, it had taken a while for the two women to get used to each other. Jen's American forthrightness had often clashed with Mona's English reserve, but as they lived and studied together, they came to a happier middle ground, at least with each other.

"He's shaken up pretty badly, looks like he was given some kind of life sentence. He hasn't said what happened yet, but I can't imagine it being anything good."

"Oh, the poor man!" Her vowels lengthen, ever so slightly, as she watches her colleague and his son enter the apartment building, the concern melting into sympathy. The accent she carried from the American South only asserts itself when she's not thinking about maintaining the more neutral accent that she has been told is more professional, or when her emotions run high or deep enough that she doesn't care what those around her think.

"Please, tell Aldous that that he can contact me if he needs anything, if there's anything I can do to lend a little aid."

"I will, and I'm sure he'll appreciate it." Mona clasps her friend's empty hand tightly. "Something tells me he's going to need all the support he can get."

In the flat, Aldous finds disarray. Furniture is overturned, and shelves are bare, with all of their contents scattered on the floor. On one wall, bright red graffiti reads "Go home, Willy Wallace!" and "Heel, Scotty Dog!" The image of a Scottish Terrier appears below the writing, snarling with bared teeth at the flat's returning occupants. Other images included penises (of many different sizes) and artists' interpretations of various rude gestures. Aldous turns Luca away from the wall and bends to his eye level. He wants to shield his son from the expression of hatred emblazoned on the wall and present in every overturned chair and ripped book page.

"Luca, go back downstairs. Ah'll be with you in a moment. I just need to grab some things, aright?" Aldous does not give Luca time to answer before he nudges him out into the hallway. He closes and locks the door behind him, engaging the chain and extra deadbolt he'd installed when he and Marta had first moved in. Ignoring the sound of Luca pounding on the door, Aldous sets about righting all of the furniture. Even though he knew that he wouldn't be in this flat long enough for this to be worth it, he needs to keep his hands busy, to have something else to focus on.

He gets lost in thought as he works. He can't let Luca stay here, especially not with him. If this is what someone, or *multiple* someones, could do when no one was home, what would they do to someone they found inside? Would it stop at graffitiing tame slurs and destroying property? Or would their malice escalate to violence, even going so far as murder? No, he can't have Luca here this week. Mona would probably take him again. She'd have custody of him until eighteen anyway, if she agreed to Aldous' plan.

Luca stops pounding on the door and sulks for a moment. He wants to help, not to be protected like a child. He doesn't want to feel like a child again, like he did when he ran away from the cops beating his father. Luca stomps down the stairs, scowling at anyone who catches his eye. He hears them whispering, muttering, murmuring to each other about his father. He hears everything from "oh, it really is a shame about Fairley. My Roddy just *adored* him and 'is class!" to "serves 'im right, the Reb bastard. Never liked 'im." This, Luca hears all too clearly. The speaker is a middle-aged man, thin on top and thick around the middle. He and his friend, a similarly built man, loiter outside. They are around the corner from Mona and Jen who, still talking out front of the building, cannot hear them. They are not, however, out of Luca's hearing. "You know what *I* say, Fred, we shoulda drove 'em out a long time ago, like we did the Fenians."

"Yeah, you said it Chuck."

"I agree." Luca's voice is calm, maybe even *too* calm. He puts his phone in his pocket after clicking a button on the side. "You really said it, didn'tcha, *Chuck*?" He approaches the two men, every step heavy with purpose. Chuck sneers at the boy. "And what *are* you saying 'served him right,' exactly? I just wanna make sure I catch your meaning properly."

Fred grabs at Chuck's arm, but he brushes Fred's hand away.

"I'm sayin' that *'ooever* I 'eard muckin' about in 'is flat, 'e 'ad the righ' idea. 'Bout time someone brought the Scotty Dog to 'eel, I say."

"Yeah?" Luca drops his head to the side. "I think you've said enough."

Luca's eyes, normally a lighter shade of brown than his father's, are dark with rage. Chuck scoffs, and Fred walks away. He does not want to be a witness of any kind to whatever follows.

"And just what do *you* plan on doin' about it?"

Chuck gets right in Luca's face, and the boy can smell the sour remnants of the man's lunch. Luca frowns and turns up his nose, the smell of malt vinegar almost too much in this close space. Chuck sees the expression change and backs up slightly. Luca lurches forward, headbutting the man in the nose. Chuck reels back, holding a hand over the bottom of his face and letting out muffled curses. Luca raises a leg and kicks Chuck in his now unguarded side. The impact shoots pain from the sole of Luca's foot all the way up to his hip. It has less effect on Chuck, but he does double over. Luca raises his hands, clasped together, over his head. With a scream that came from deep inside, he tries to bring them down on Chuck's head, but someone catches hold of his wrist from behind.

"Luca, what are you doing?" Mona turns him around to face her, and she notices Chuck trying to slip away. "Sir, please stay here until we can get everything figured out, please."

"Fat chance!" Chuck stands up straight. Jen runs around the corner, following Mona. "Your brat just attacked me outta nowhere!"

"He was talkin' shite about Dad!" Luca yells. His voice is just Scottish enough that Chuck can hear it, and he sneers. "He was sayin' that whoever tossed our flat was right, that we shouldn't be allowed in the Empire. I've got it recorded!" Luca holds up his phone and clicks the record button again, stopping the recording. Chuck freezes in his spot.

"Wait, back up. *What* happened in your flat?" Jen asks. She looks between Mona and Luca.

"It was trashed, all the furniture turned over, Dad's books ripped, stuff painted on the walls." Luca is crying now, his righteous anger too much for his body to handle without some kind of expression. "An' he said something that was on the wall."

"What did he say?"

Mona holds Luca's shoulders and tries to get him to look at her. He just sobs, a pitiful sound that he'd had far too much reason for these days. She turns on Chuck.

"What did you say?" Her voice is low, angry, and every word emphasized. Chuck is silent, just opening and closing his mouth as if willing *any* noise to come out that would defend him.

"He said," Luca speaks again, through the sobs that wrack his body, "that it was about time someone brought the-" He hesitates. Words like this have never passed his lips before, and he wishes they didn't have to now. "The 'Scotty Dog' to heel."

"What?"

Mona's voice somehow sounds lower, and there's a flatness to her tone that Jen knows to be *very* dangerous. The last time she heard that question, with this inflection, was when their dean had refused to discipline a student who'd harassed several of their classmates because of his family's connections. That dean, as far as she knows, was never able to find a job in education again after Mona's report ripped him to shreds and led to his dismissal. Chuck had never heard this question, with this inflection, but he somehow knows just by hearing it that he will be lucky to come out of this interaction in one piece.

"Look, miss, I didn't-"

"No. You, be silent, now." Chuck's mouth closes before he thinks to close it himself. Mona stares into Chuck's eyes, green piercing into dull blue. "Luca, dear, can I see your phone? I just want to check everyone's story." Luca puts his phone into her outstretched hand. She does not break eye contact with Chuck. "Go with Mrs. Caldwel. I'll meet you around front in a bit, alright?" She still does not break eye contact with Chuck.

Jen takes hold of Luca's shoulder and leads him away. For a while, he can hear the recording play, then his aunt's raised voice. By that point, he is too far away to make out any words, but he can tell that she is angry. He has never heard her raise her voice except to be heard, and the fury that radiates from around the corner sends a chill down his spine. Jen brings Luca to a bench and sits beside him, unsure whether to reach out and comfort him or leave him be. He answers that question for her by throwing his arms around her neck and sobbing. She rubs circles into his back, rocking him slightly, and leans her head against the top of his. After a while, she speaks gently.

"Hey, it's gonna be okay. I've known your aunt for a *long* time, and I know she's gonna handle this guy with no problem."

"But it's not just *this* guy, is it?" Luca straightens and wipes the tears from his face. "It's his friend, and the Academy parents, and everyone who saw the news story and believed it without a question." He balls his fists. "It's the people who look at me with pity, or with *disgust*, when they hear Dad talk or hear who he is! It's *everyone* except us four, and I *hate* it!" Luca stands, pacing and flexing his fingers.

"What do you mean, 'us four'?" Jen is bewildered as she watches her student pace.

"You, me, Dad, and Auntie Mona." The reply, though short and obviously annoyed, warms Jen's heart nonetheless. Luca still paces, stalking back and forth on the pavement and alternating his hands between fists and flat. This is how Mona finds him when she approaches, through raw from ensuring that she will haunt Chuck's nightmares for at least a Fisian season. She looks to Jen for an explanation, but Aldous interrupts her before she can begin by approaching and speaking first.

"Aah, I assume Luca has already told ye 'bout the flat." He observes Luca's movements, watching him expel the pent-up anger. "Ah've handled some of it, but it's a lot for one person t'handle."

"Don't worry, you can both stay with me," Mona croaks. She eyes the suitcase in Aldous' wake. "As long as you need to. You need help clearing out?"

"Probably, but that can wait until tomorrow. Righ' now, I need to tell you all what happened."

The drive, like the earlier one from the police station, is silent. Aldous sits in the passenger seat. Luca sits in the back, trying to catch his father's eye in the rear-view mirror. Aldous stares straight forward. Jen follows in her own car. When they arrive at Mona's house, they gather in the den. No one speaks for a moment, until Jen does.

"Why don't I make us some tea? I'll go start the kettle." She rises, walking out of the tension. Aldous clears his throat, then looks up at Luca.

"There's no easy way to say this, so Ah'll just say it, I suppose." He takes a deep breath and closes his eyes. "In a week, I leave for Fisian Moon 1. I've been given what they call a 'specialized assignment,' told to study some machine so we can mass-produce it."

A crash sounds from the kitchen. He opens his eyes to see Luca and Mona in shock. Jen walks into the doorway, visibly shaken. She remembers an all too similar conversation with her husband after he returned from the police station. Before he was transported. The last time she saw him.

The rest of the story spills out before Aldous can stop it. He barely breathes in the retelling. His audience hangs on his every word.

"And there's nothing we can do to fight it?" Luca asks, looking between Mona and Aldous for the tiniest morsel of hope.

"It was Chief Constable Edwards herself that told me. Apparently, they wanted me in a position where Ah couldnae refuse, thus the severe beating and smear campaign. They ensured that Ah winnae be able to stay here long, and that Ah winnae have a job tae keep me here."

"So," Mona says, "what's your plan?"

"Tomorrow, Ah'll go back tae the flat an' get everything out that I can, then start preparin' tae leave."

January 27th

Aldous squeezes Luca as tightly as he can. Luca squeezes back, wishing this was enough to keep his father earthbound. A chime sounds over the station's PA system.

"Attention passengers: flight FM1-537 will be departing in ten minutes. Nee-poex foestai F-M-loehuh qui-pai-spehuh, naehuh-kimtal."

"You should probably get going," Mona says. "Don't wanna hold up the workings of Unified Britain." As Aldous and Luca release each other, she puts a hand on Aldous' shoulder. "As much as it's possible, don't worry. We'll meet you right here when you come back, alright?"

"Aright." Aldous picks up his duffle bag. It is strange for him to think that he would be gone for at least a decade, and yet that he would only need a few days' worth of supplies. It seems like such a waste of time and resources. "Luca, ye listen well to your aunt, yeah? Ah'll send a message as soon as Ah can. I promise." Luca nods. He can't speak around the lump in his throat.

He has known that this moment would arrive for a week now, but that doesn't make the moment itself any easier to get through. He tries to be strong, though, for his father's sake. Luca doesn't want his father's last memory of him to be him crying. Aldous reaches for a hug, but hesitates. He settles for ruffling Luca's curls and kissing him on the forehead.

Aldous follows the signs to the platform he'd been told to find. When he arrives, he stops short and nearly slips on the slick floor.

The starsailor looms above him, easily five times his height. Its front end, designed to cut through atmospheres, tapers to a point like a jouster's lance. The rest of the starsailor is metallic bulk, wide and tall to accommodate the Cryo pods and engine works. The hull shines with the polish that the crew just finished applying. The silvery finish dazzles Aldous so much that, for just a moment, he forgets the gloom hanging over him and allows a touch of excitement to enter his heart. The spark goes out as soon as it appears, however, as Aldous sees the guards on the platform. They remind him of why he's here, and the gloom settles back in. One of the guards, a young woman with dark skin and tightly braided hair, notices him enter the platform. She approaches him with a wide smile.

"Mr. Fairley! Thank you for joining us so punctually." Her eyes are mismatched; one is a rich, deep brown, while the other is a shocking, bright violet. "I'm Leftenant Frasier. If you'll follow me, I'll show you where to stow your baggage and pick up your Cryogear." She gestures toward the back of the starsailor, and Aldous follows her as she begins to walk. "Do you have any questions about the craft, sir? I noticed you perk up a little at seeing it, thought talking about it might ease your mind."

"I appreciate the thought, but Ah dinnae have any questions." Frasier nods, and they walk the rest of the sailor's length in silence. When they reach the rear, she gestures to an open compartment.

"There should be a section of this labelled with your name. That's where you should stow your bag. And if you look over that way," Frasier indicates an area of the wall opposite the sailor, "you'll see the Cryogear. It's also labelled with your name."

"Thank ye, Leftenant Frasier."

"You're welcome, Mr. Fairley. Once you've put on your Cryogear, just come aboard." She returns to her post, leaving Aldous to his own devices.

He stows his bag in the labelled compartment, then turns to the Cryogear wall. He finds his suit and other supplies, as well as a changing stall, with ease. After removing his own clothing, he steps into the deep purple coveralls and black foot coverings. As he walks back to his bag to stow the clothes he had changed out of, he pulls up the hood to cover his head. He then continues to the middle of the sailor, where the guards are standing in front of an open hatch. They step aside, and he steps into the ship that will take him away from his home.

"Welcome, Al-dous Fair-ley." An automated voice greets him as he steps into the main area of the ship. "Once you enter your Cryopod, your mission briefing will begin."

"Righ'. Thanks." Aldous answers stiffly, and he hears at least one of the guards behind him snickering. A Cryopod opens before him and spills ice-blue light into the otherwise dark room. Inside is a cushioned surface, tilted just enough so that his weight will not be on his feet for the entire journey. The cushions look brand new, the white fabric shimmering slightly in the light. He looks around, trying to see if anyone else is aboard. All he sees are other Cryopods, some still dark and some dimly lit, allowing Aldous to see their occupants. All of them are dressed the same as he is, faces covered with the same kind of apparatus that will cover Aldous' face once the freezing process begins, protecting it from the harsh cold. He steps into the open pod, settling himself on the cushioned backrest. The lights lower as the pod door shuts. On the inside of the door, a video feed appears. He sees the face of Chief Constable Edwards, a seemingly genuine smile on her face. The same automated voice from before speaks again.

"Begin mission briefing." The video feed stutters for a moment, and then Chief Constable Edwards begins to speak.

"Good morning, Mr. Fairley. I know you will be departing soon, so I will keep this briefing…well, *brief*." She lets out a chuckle, proud of her minor word play. "This is the machine you will be studying."

An image replaces her face. In it, Aldous sees a machine on a factory floor, one that looks a bit like the toy robot he had as a child. It is arranged roughly in the shape of a Fisian, with a head, torso, and two sets of arms. The head is a cube with a screen in the center of the face that is turned toward the camera. The screen is blank in the photo. The torso is like a stretched cube, unadorned except for the arms. The arms are cylindrical, and they end in five-fingered hands. In the image, one hand holds something up to the screen. There must be a sensor array behind or around the screen that scan whatever the machine holds up to it. The other hands are empty, but one is already reaching for the next object to come down the line. The torso reaches to the floor.

"The name its inventor gave it was 'Hleh*click*de Tisk'Ah.' Our Fisian colleagues have translated that to 'Miracle Metal' in English. We do not know if there is some cultural connotation of which we are unaware, or if there is no significance to the name, but I digress." The image of the machine disappears and is replaced with the Chief Constable's face once more. "Your mission is to analyze this machine, inside and out, so that British and Fisian factories throughout the combined empires can implement the same technology and increase their productivity in the same way that Fisian Moon 1's facility has. Our goal is mimicry and mass production. You will report to Supervisor Thoon-Vai once you arrive on site."

A small image of the Supervisor appears, just large enough for Aldous to see violet skin and dark hair. The image is rough. He will have to ask for confirmation of the Supervisor's appearance when he wakes up.

"You will also submit your final report to them. Once you have done so, and they have recorded satisfaction with your report's thoroughness, you will be cleared to return to Earth." The Supervisor's image disappears. Chief Constable Edwards smiles. "Best of luck to you, Aldous." The video feed disappears. Aldous hears the mask apparatus start to descend from above him. It settles over his face, and the automated voice comes through again.

"Commencing Cryofreeze protocol in three. Two. One. Commencing."

The air inside the pod gets colder and colder. The air coming through the mask smells sweet. It makes Aldous feel drowsy, feel like he's floating in the clouds. As he fades away into sleep, he thinks of Marta. With his wife's face on his mind, Aldous falls into Cryosleep.

CHAPTER TWO

Adthe breathes in, the cold atmosphere filling her lungs. The door closes behind her with a gentle swish. She raises the top set of arms over her head, interlocking her fingers so that she gets the greatest stretch possible. She does the same with her lower arms, pushing them out in front of her. She groans as she looks around, taking in her complex in the few rays of light shed from the Atmodome on the first moon. All around, she sees run-down buildings whose tops crumbled long ago. Only the lower floors are habitable now, but no one requisitions repairs anymore. They do not want to hear the same chorus of "We must care for the human prisoners! If the Atmodome fails, then what will we do? We would love to help, but our hands are tied!" Some who worked on the Atmodome when construction first started, like Adthe's father, said that it was the most solid structure they had ever seen. Even now, just over a season later, the dome has not required a single repair. Still, the Hu'Tu who live here make do. They use salvageable materials from collapses to make their own repairs.

"Leek'ah!" Adthe's brother, Raht, calls out to her mind. *"Kee'poe'doohuh'nnee'ah?"*

"Com'ing!"

Adthe jogs to catch up with her twin. They wear matching baggy coveralls, the uniform required by their workplace, and close-cropped haircuts. The only way one would be able to differentiate between the two on first glance would be to examine their facial expressions. Raht always looks angry, at least a little bit. His brow is regularly furrowed, and his nostrils flare in order to vent the heat of frustration that grips his heart as he watches the Fisians rule over the

Hu'Tu. Adthe, on the other hand, usually wears a calmer, kinder expression. Though she has seen the ways that the Fisians have kept her people down, she still believes what her father did; she believes that it can't be too long until someone rises to fight against the Fisians and drive them out of power. Who that person would be, Hu'Tu, Human, or even Fisian, matters less to her than knowing that they will come one day.

Raht and Adthe jog through the swirling, shifting atmospheric fog that surrounds them, passing by decrepit buildings and broken-down transports on both sides of their path. The old surface-speeders and starsailors loom tall over the twins as they come closer to the shuttleport. Many of the machines look skeletal now, with parts of the hulls and interiors alike being scavenged by mechanics and inventors over the years. She stops beside one of them, the starsailor that had provided the screen she needed to construct the prototype of her little miracle. Well, it's not so little now, she thinks.

"Hu'Tu worker, approach the shuttleport or be left behind!" A Fisian man, one of the lower supervisors, yells at Adthe. She breaks out of her reminiscence and runs toward the shuttleport door.

"Kee'zhoo'hleh-"

"Save your apologies, worker. And read the sign!" The Fisian points above his head at a sign that Adthe had not noticed yet.

Hu'Tu ki-Leh K. ki-Leh ng-Lɪʃ nœ fi-ʒən nœ ni-ðe-ɾe wedʒ æ.

NO HU-TU TO BE SPOKEN. ENGLISH OR FISIAN ONLY, ON PENALTY OF WAGE

DIMINISHMENT.

For a moment, Adthe looks exactly like her brother. But she bites her tongue and closes her eyes, breathing in the last taste of cold air she will have until her workday is done.

"Un'der'stood." She walks past the Fisian and into the shuttleport. She finds Raht just inside the door.

"*English it is, dear sister!*" Raht nudges her with one of his lower elbows as he talks in his mind. "*I know I would rather kiss a xah'loo than speak like they do.*"

"*Just be careful, brother. I cannot lose you too.*" Adthe examines her brother's face. The anger is stronger now, his brow set low over his eyes.

"*You will not.*" He sets a hand on his sister's shoulder. "*Kee'stom'nnee'ah.*"

A tone sounds over the PA system, and the door to the shuttle opens swiftly. Adthe files in behind her brother and the others, ending up nearest to the door. As soon as she steps on, the door closes just as swiftly as it opens, with enough force behind it that she counted all of her fingers to ensure that none had been caught. The shuttle lurches and takes her stomach with it, and she clings to the metal loop hanging above her head. Even in her second week, she has not gotten used to the lurching of the shuttle upon takeoff.

She looks out the small window in the door. She has not gotten used to the view from the atmosphere yet, either. She smiles as the shuttle passes by the rings of her home planet, weaving in between the chunks of ice and rock trapped in orbit. The moon's surface grows closer and closer, and all too soon the shuttle lurches to a stop. As soon as it touches down, a door opens on the opposite side of the shuttle. The workers file out in the same order they filed in, making Adthe the last to enter the Hu'Tu entrance. She clambers up to her spot at the observation station, perilously perched on a catwalk that is barely wide enough for the computer terminals that had been set up here.

Already at his seat is Liam, Adthe's work partner. As she slips her earpiece in, Liam gives her a cheery wave. His smile is contagious, so she returns it with a shy wave of her own.

Adthe's smile disappears when a shrill beep comes through her earpiece, causing her to cringe and turn away from Liam.

"Worker Xi'Adthe, please report to the control office immediately." The message comes through her earpiece, the rough voice piercing to the center of her hearing. As she stands, her partner notices.

"Everything alright?" Liam sees the remnant of the wince on Adthe's face, and his own brow softens in compassion.

"Ah. Yes." Adthe switches off the screen at her station and points toward the control office windows. "Su'per'vi'sor calls." She wishes she had more confidence with English, but everything comes out so halting that most of the other English speakers lose patience with her easily.

"Oh, how *lovely*. Give them my best, won't you?" Liam's deadpan delivery in his drawling Australian accent usually makes Adthe laugh, even if only a little, but not today. Today, she is concerned. Why would the Supervisor call for her? Had she done something wrong? If so, it is nothing that she is aware of. But the Supervisor *did* sound angry.

Adthe climbs down the ladder from her observation station. She walks past her brother as he shovels fuel into the Melter, focusing hard on her body temperature so that it does not spike too high. She does not understand how Raht and his partner can work so close to so hot a flame without collapsing, and it always worries her when she sees him step back and wipe his brow in the few moments that he is not under Vai's direct observation.

Adthe looks up to see where the scrap falls into the Melter, seemingly dropping in from some kind of void in the sky. As she rushes past, the red-gold streams of molten metal flow into ingots and molds, depending on what output is needed that day. Today, it is ingots, as blocks can be shaped and stamped to fit any mold after the fact, and there is too much of a variety on deck today. The ingots glow for a moment, but the metal within cools almost immediately upon meeting the air. Though it is warmed by the Melter, the factory still bears the chill of the outside moon. Despite this, the metal still holds just enough heat to create a fog around the cooling barrels when the finished shapes are dunked into them.

Adthe passes by the last aspect of the factory line and can't resist taking a look up at it. The Hleh‡de Tisk'Ah stands tall, at least twice as tall as Adthe herself. It scans finished pieces and displays either the Fisian symbol "æ" on a green field or "Ŧ" on a red one to show whether or not it has passed inspection. The light arms move fluidly, contrasting the dark, solid metal of the body. As soon as one scan is complete, the machine picks up the next piece that comes down the line. The operation is smooth and efficient.

"Worker Xi'Adthe, is there a problem with the machine?" Vai's voice comes through again, making Adthe look up to the observation window. The Supervisor stood in plain view, both sets of arms crossed.

"No 'ro'lem. I come." Adthe rushes up the stairs to the control office, taking them two at a time. She pushes open the door to the control office and sees not only the Supervisor standing before her, but a Human man that she has never seen before. He is tall, even by Hu'Tu standards, and has dark brown skin. She can see no hair on his head. He's wearing something that looks like a suit, but was not a color Adthe was used to seeing suits in. This suit is a shade of green mixed with brown, with polished gold buttons running down the middle of the coat. A brown belt runs across his waist and from one shoulder down to the hip. The trousers are the same color as the coat, and he wears shoes that match his belt almost perfectly. The shoes are just a shade darker.

He carries a hat under his arm that looks like it is dark blue, but Adthe cannot tell for sure because of the shadow on it.

"Xi'Adthe, this is Major General Cavanaugh of the United British Army." Vai bristles at having to make this introduction, and this does not get past Adthe. She notices, but is still bewildered. The man puts his hand out to shake hers, and she accepts it hesitantly. "I do not know why, but he has asked to see you."

"I'm here because of that, oh, what did you say she called it, Johnston?" General Cavanaugh turns to a man that Adthe had not noticed. As dark as the general's skin is, Johnston's is pale; he is slighter than the general, but has much more hair than his superior officer. The hair is dark and wavy, near black with a violet tint in the bright light.

"Ah, she called it the Hlehǂde Tisk'Ah." Johnston turns to look at Adthe. "Is that correct?"

"Yes."

"And, what would that be in English, do you know?" General Cavanaugh looks at everyone around him.

Vai stays silent. They are surveying the scene with a bitter expression. If it had been up to them, this machine would never have been installed at this facility, no matter its English name. They watch Adthe look to the ground, either trying to puzzle out a translation or ashamed that she cannot come up with one. The thought brings a superior smirk to Vai's face. After a moment, Johnston breaks the silence.

"Best I can tell, the literal translation would be Hleh*click*de: Miracle, and Tisk'Ah: Metal."

"That sounds about right," Vai scoffs. They know how much of an upstart Raht is, how *proud* he is of his people's so-called accomplishments, so it's no surprise whatsoever to Vai that his sister would be similarly vain.

"I think that is right." Adthe hesitates. She can feel Vai's disdain for her, but she continues after a moment of considering what to say. "What can I tell you?"

"Well," the general answers, looking a bit uncomfortable, "we don't have questions for you, so to speak. I'm here to inform you that we are bringing in a roboticist to study your machine in the hopes that we can replicate it."

Adthe is silent. They want to make more of her machine, *her* creation, without asking her questions? Do they think that their roboticist can understand the Hlehǂde Tisk'Ah better than the one who built it, who programmed it, who spent days in her common room testing different strings of code until she found just the one she wanted? Why would they take her out of the process?

"Why are you silent, Worker Xi?" Vai questions, their voice even harsher than usual. "Is this not wonderful news? Your machine has attracted governmental attention." The smirk returns as they watch Adthe try to restrain her emotions. Anger, disbelief, disappointment, they all flash across the Hu'Tu's face, filling her bruise-like skin with more and more pink and red. She breathes, trying to regain control over her body temperature.

"There are so ma'ny things I could say. I have to find the words." She breathes again, buying herself a moment more to process her emotions. "If I can hel' your ro'ot'i'cist, was it?" Johnston nods. "If I can hel', I will. If they need my notes, to ask que'stions, I will hel'." Vai looks sour again. Adthe tries to smile.

"Well, isn't that delightful!" The general is stiff, still uncomfortable from the situation. "I'm sure they will appreciate your offer. For now, I recommend you return to your station. We don't want your partner to have all of the work on *his* plate, now do we?" He goes from stiff to talking to Adthe as if she is a child. She bristles at this, but tries to hide it as much as possible.

"Of course." She nods to the general and Johnston, then to Supervisor Thoon. She turns away and lets her emotions out. She hears a small voice at the back of her mind.

"*Gyee'ruh'le'uhng?*" Her brother is curious. He must have seen her go to the control office. She looks over to the Melter, and sees him still hard at work.

"*Nee'too'kuh'nnee'ah.*" She does not have time to discuss the meeting now, not even in her mind. She has to return to work. She barely notices anything as she walks back to the observation tower. She does, however, feel like someone is watching her. When she turns to look, she sees no one. The only thing behind her is her miracle machine.

2037

Afternoon, "Springtime"

Fisian Moon One

Adthe looks again at the writing displayed on the Hleh‡de Tisk'Ah's screen. She understands the words well enough, but why her machine is asking the question is unclear at best.

ki'rry jəng? Why am I?

How could this be happening? Adthe could tell the machine its purpose, what she had built it for, but it should not have enough awareness to know that it exists, let alone to ask why. She decides to answer while continuing to test the translation protocols that she was running.

"Gyee'hi'nnee yuh'ung daht'ah'yuh hee'hleh. Can you trans'late that?" On the screen, she sees a circle of white circles, spinning around a central point on the otherwise blank screen. After a moment, the display shows text.

<u>"(I) made you because my brother to help." ɟi'Sa Hlyng? Did I do right?</u>

Adthe frowns. That did not look like it would have come from an English speaker, but from a dictionary or too literal a translation. Something must have gone wrong with the program. As Adthe turns to stop the subroutine, the screen clears.

"Tisk'Ah'hun? What is wrong?" After the question leaves her lips, the screen repopulates.

<u>"ɟi'Hɪ'Ni jə'əng DAt'æ'jœ Hɪ'Hle" means "I made you to help my brother."</u>
<u>ki'Sa Hly'æng? Is it correct now?</u>

Adthe's jaw drops. She did not expect the machine to correct itself like that. She looks back to the code, trying to find what line instructed it to do that. She finds nothing in her input logs. She does, however, find something in the system-generated commands.

"How did you do that?" The orbiting circles return to the Hleh‡de Tisk'Ah's display. After a moment, the circles are replaced by text.

<u>ɟi'Hɪ'Ni'qu ni'ɢAzd'æng? You built me to learn, yes?</u>

"I gave you learn'ing, yes, 'ut not for this." Adthe runs a hand through her short amethyst hair absentmindedly, smearing grease through it. "I gave you learn'ing so you could hel' my daht'ah, not to teach your'self new things."

"Addie, everythin' alright?" Liam's brow knits with worry. Adthe has been spending more and more time with her machine, to the point where the Supervisor tends to watch and time her. Thankfully, the past couple of weeks have been pretty calm as far as breakages or malfunctions go, aside from the Hleh‡de Tisk'Ah acting a bit quirky at times.

Adthe does not answer him, instead focusing on the screen in front of her. On it is a single word, in both Hu'Tu and English: why? Liam had told her of Earth creatures called "toddlers," and how they were full of the same kind of questions that her machine is asking her now. Did she somehow create a toddler?

"Li'am, it is ask'ing me ques'tions. Questions about itself. It is like a todd'ler. What do I do?" She looks at Liam, but hears nothing. He looks thoughtful, and Adthe's gaze drifts back to the machine. Worry creeps in. What if this is a sign that something was broken in her machine? How can she fix a problem that she cannot see? She does not hear Liam's answer, if he gives one, as she processes what has happened. She can only think one thing: what happens when the roboticist finds out about this? What will he do to her creation?

"Addie? Can you hear me?" Adthe flinches and snaps back to looking at Liam, eyes wide and shining with unshed tears. "I'll take that as a no. I said, if it's like a toddler, then I guess that really does make it a little miracle, eh?"

2040

Morning, Nearing the end of "Springtime"

Fisian Moon One

Adthe doesn't want to admit this, to herself or anyone else, but she wishes that no one had sent for the roboticist. For the last five earth years, she has dreaded arriving at the factory for her shifts. It has only gotten more intense the closer the arrival date becomes. She fears that she will arrive for her shift and find someone poking around her creation. She wants to explain the machine, to help their analyst understand it, and to keep them from understanding *too* much.

There are things about it that even *she* does not fully understand yet, and she has not had the opportunity to study it in-depth because Vai will not allow her to stay at the station for too long or to take the core home for analysis.

"How do we know that you will not tamper with the machine before the roboticist comes?" The Supervisor had asked this question every time Adthe so much as implied that she would like to run even the most basic diagnostics on the machine on her own. "I know how desperately you want to be involved in this, Worker Xi, but sabotage is out of the question, and I cannot be too careful. Not with your, well, *family history*."

That jab, delivered several shifts ago, rings in Adthe's ears even now. As she enters the shuttleport and feels the rush of hot air from the shuttle's engine, she is grateful that it will disguise the angry flush to her cheeks. Why should it matter that her brother runs his mouth about changing things when Vai knows as well as she does that he's in no position to actually act on his rants? Why should her father's supposed crimes, committed over a quarter of a season ago, make any difference in Adthe's trustworthiness? It's not like she's trying to incite rebellion. She just wants to understand why her machine's behavior seems to be changing, only slightly, when she can find nothing in the code to explain it. She wants to make sure that the roboticist doesn't find something that will make them take her creation away.

The view outside the shuttle holds no draw for her now, and she stares straight ahead. Her mind holds just one thought, repeating over and over and over again. Today, if it does not behave, she could lose her miracle. Forever.

She makes her way up to the observation station, climbing slowly up the ladder as her thoughts still swirl in dread. When she reaches the top and switches on the computer in front of her, she looks out over the factory floor, all dark metal with bright fire soon to come. She relishes the moment of quiet before everything starts, before she has to put in her earpiece, before anything can go wrong. The Melter starts, fuel shoveled into its mouth and spark set onto the fuel. It roars to life, as do the conveyor belts that bring the metal from station to station. Noise fills what had been a silent place.

The Human prisoners, all in bright orange clothing, filter in through their entrance. Liam looks up to see Adthe already at the observation station, computer switched on. He smiles. That girl is going to work herself into the ground if she's not careful. If he was in charge of things here, she would be up in the control office, handling the more intricate problems that arise here, rather than a simple technician. He knows what she is capable of, and it makes him proud to work with her, but it also makes his blood boil to see how much the Supervisor and the government that they represent keep brilliant Hu'Tu like Adthe down on ground level when they have more mind power than those in control. He pushes those thoughts aside as he climbs the ladder and smiles at his partner.

"Gooood morning, Addie! Today should be the day, yeah?" He puts a hand on her shoulder and feels how tense it is. She stares straight ahead, fixing her vision on the Hleɫdeh Tisk'Ah.

"Li'am, what if they want to kill it?" Adthe's face is devoid of emotional display, but her voice shakes. She breathes deeply, trying to rein in the tremble. "What if Supervisor Thoon knows? What if-"

"What if I grow another set of arms? What if I jump up on the desk and start singin' opera?" Adthe looks at Liam, unsure if she should be confused or annoyed. She settles on both. He squeezes her shoulder, and turns her chair so that she looks at him. "The roboticist is just here to study your little miracle, nothing more. Whatever happens next, we can tackle it when it comes. No sense in getting so worked up over it that Vai notices your stress and decides to use it." He releases her shoulder and ruffles her hair. "Remember, you're not doing this alone. You've got me in your corner, and your brother. And, if this guy knows his shit, he'll be on your side, too. You've created something incredible, and any expert on robotics'll know that right away."

"That is what I fear," Adthe says. She rakes her fingers through her hair to settle it and returns to her focus, watching for any malfunctions throughout the factory system. Her eyes occasionally drift to her machine, just long enough to confirm that it is still working as it should. Though it has no mechanism for showing emotion, she could almost swear that it looks happy as it works, swinging its arms to pick up, scan, and deposit the first few parts coming down the line in the appropriate bins for passing inspection for the different forms used. She shifts her focus rapidly, first on the screen in front of her, then on the other aspects of the factory workings, then sticking on her machine before she shakes herself free of its draw and starts the cycle again. Every time she looks back at the Hlełdeh Tisk'Ah, she sees it look a little more alive, a little more happy, a little more-

"Addie, you alright?" Liam's voice pulls Adthe out of her focused state. She shakes her head, clearing away the worry that had crept back in. she looks down at the computer display. No issues detected in the system. She looks out onto the factory floor. She, again, sees no issues. She breathes out a sigh, cold enough that Liam feels the chill and shivers. She turns to her partner and sees the worry etched into the sun lines on his face. She tries to smile, and is about half successful.

"I am sor'ry to scare you. I am fine. Are you o'kay?" Liam nods, then stands and turns off his monitor.

"I have to go. I've been asked to meet the roboticist at the shuttleport, act as the factory's welcoming committee." He rolls his eyes, which makes Adthe chuckle. "Why they aren't sending one of the non-prisoners, I dunno, but I'm off. I'll see you when I get back, make introductions, all that." He stretches his arms behind his back, then starts off down the ladder to the factory floor. "Man, I am *not* looking forward to that first step out the door! Opening the Atmodome for the starsailor probably let in a bloody artic breeze, and it'll take me *ages* to thaw when I get back!"

2040

January 21ˢᵗ

The thawing process is *deeply* unpleasant. Bright lights flood Aldous' vision and he squints, every bit of light feeling like a needle stabbing into his eyes and brain. Aldous becomes all too aware of the tube in his nose that is supposed to help him breathe as he comes back to room temperature. He wants to rip it out so it will stop tickling the back of his nasal cavity, but he doesn't even get his hand up off of the table before an automated voice breaks through the silence.

"Please do not remove the breathing tube. Doing so prematurely may damage your nasal pathways."

"Arigh', fine." Aldous leans back and tries to relax while the ship-board computer makes its scans. "Can ye turn the lights down? They're a wee bit intense for just waking up!"

The computer makes no answer, and he closes his eyes in an effort to dull the light's impact. His skin feels like it's on fire, itching and burning as the numbness wears off. But he makes every effort not to scratch, as he is sure that doing so will only invoke the ire of the robotic voice. His eyes were so dry upon first waking, but they feel a bit better in that respect after about ten minutes of being able to blink again. He probably should have closed his eyes before the Cryofreeze started, but it's too late to do anything about that now. The table is warm, probably *only* warm, but it feels like it's searing into his frozen skin. He squirms, trying to find some level of relief from the discomfort, the pain, but it only exposes more of his skin to the table. He grits his teeth and tries to hold back a groan.

"First Cryo, eh?" The voice comes from beside Aldous. He turns his head and opens his eyes, blinding lights be damned. He sees a young man on a similar table. His eyes bear the same shine of recently relieved dryness that Aldous' do, but they are a bright, grassy green. His skin is light, but not so pale as to appear sickly.

"Wha' gave it away?" Aldous grimaces as his cheek burns. It also itches from the stubble that somehow still grew while all of his other bodily functions were stalled. Hopefully, he'll get to shave soon.

"The twitching. I had it bad my first time, too." The young man smiles. His voice is smooth, posh, and utterly calm. He is so still that if his eyes were closed, someone might think he was still asleep. "The name's Michael. Michael Robinson. I'd shake your hand, but…"

"Ah know. The warden's watchin', aye?"

"Yeah," Michael says with a light laugh. He looks like he can't be any older than twenty, thirty at the most, but he bears the Cryo thaw like a seasoned professional.

"If ye don' mind me askin', how many times have ye been thawed out like this?" Aldous quirks his eyebrow, then grimaces at the skin pulling on his forehead. Michael laughs again, more to himself, and takes a moment before he answers.

"This'll be time number three. This is only my second trip off-planet, but I had a decent bit of training before this trip to get me used to the feeling. Nothing quite like spending over an hour in the Arctic snow and then immediately getting into a sauna with the rest of my unit. No one leaves, everyone's miserable, so we find ways to make it bearable."

"Ye're military?" Aldous has so much of his focus devoted to the conversation that he barely registers the burning anymore. He also doesn't notice that the lights have finally dimmed, or that a robotic hand has removed the nasal tube.

"Yes, Army. It's my first tour off-planet. I'll be on FM 1 for at least five years before I come home, do this all again."

"First tour? Then what was your first *trip* off-planet?"

Michael's smile falters, the question triggering a memory he hadn't thought about in a while.

"My dad was pretty big in manufacturing and architecture, back when he was still around. He helped design a lot of the human spaces on FM one, including the Atmodome itself. When it was completed, he was invited to come and tour the facilities he'd designed and he brought me along. He'd always wanted me to follow his path, take over the company, and figured that a ten year old could handle Cryo just fine."

A bit of bitterness creeps into Michael's voice during the story, as well as sorrow.

"He left the business to me when he passed, expected me to just carry on with it as he'd done. I passed ownership to my brothers and joined up as soon as I hit eighteen. *Developmentally* eighteen, that is."

A tone sounds from the PA system, and Michael sits up, stretching his arms over his head and rolling his neck. Aldous feels no more burning, and he sits up as well.

"Ten years off planet, most of it in suspended animation, means that I'm older on a timeline than I am in my body. When I came home from that first trip, I was legally twenty, even though I was only ten in mind and body. We got it adjusted, but that meant that everyone I'd grown up with to that point was in Uni or running their parents' businesses. I missed ten years just because my father wanted me on a damn publicity tour."

Michael stands, continuing to stretch. Aldous does the same, his joints creaking and popping with every step he takes toward the dark blue-green jumpsuit hanging beside the door. The inside was plaid, black and white lines on a field of berry red. He touches the lining, feeling the wool tartan fabric. It's his family's tartan. As he pulled it off of the hanger, he thought of Luca, who would be about eighteen now back on Earth. Is he talking about Aldous with this kind of bitterness? Talking to someone, maybe Mona, maybe a partner, about the fact that he's losing ten years of life with his father? Does he blame Aldous?

"Please exit the evaluation chamber." The automated voice makes Aldous jump, and Michael laughs heartily.

"Penny for your thoughts?" Michael touches the older man lightly on the shoulder, already dressed in his army uniform. Aldous smiles, but it doesn't reach his eyes.

"What ye said about your da got me thinkin' about my own son. He'd be about your age now, turned eighteen a few months back. For me, it's been a blink, but for him it's already been half a decade. Even if Ah go home tomorrow, he'll still be a grown man, out of Uni if he decides to go, by the time Ah get back." He tears up, but tries to stop them from flowing. "Ah just hope he disnae hate me for leavin'."

"You were pressed into service, right?" Michael sees the bewildered expression on Aldous' face. "We were given a briefing on the transport's passengers before we departed," he explains. He puts his hand firmly on Aldous' shoulder. "If your son hates anyone right now, it is likely the people who took you from him, not you. You didn't ask for this assignment, and I'm sure they didn't exactly make it *easy* to refuse." He looks around, then leans in closer to Aldous'

ear and whispers. "He's learned early that the United British and Fisian Governments don't

actually care about their citizenry, only how they can further their own interests. He's probably

thanking you for that lesson."

Michael straightens up and exits the room, leaving Aldous in a muddle of emotions.

As he walks out of the chamber, he stews over everything that Michael had said. Had

none of his superior officers noticed any of these sentiments? Aldous walks down the corridor to

the main chamber of the ship, the last thing he remembered seeing before going into Cryo. A

group of people are milling about, all of them in clusters of conversation. Some IPos guard

prisoners in bright orange jumpsuits and leg restraints. Michael stands with a group of identically

uniformed people, bundled up in parkas and thick gloves. Aldous looks down at his jumpsuit and

wonders just how thick the wool lining is, and how well it will protect him. One of the army unit,

a woman with graying brown hair tied into a severe bun, approaches him.

"Mr. Fairley, I am Lance Corporal Hall, and my section will be your escort while you are

on this mission." She indicates Michael and the others. "Let's go ahead and get introductions

over with." She moves with the same kind of forthrightness that laces her voice, no doubt a result

of her American upbringing. Aldous hears a faint accent, one that he thinks comes from the

northeast of that country. "I hear you've already had a chance to meet Private Robinson, so I

won't reintroduce you." Michael gives a cheeky wave, ending it before his section leader could

see him. "This is Ivarsson, Jenkins, Kapoor, and Li." As each soldier is indicated, they give a

short nod. Aldous nods and tries to smile at each of them.

"Good morning. Actually, is it morning?"

"Approximately fourteen-hundred hours GMT, sir." Ivarsson stands at stiff attention, but makes eye contact with Aldous. "Though I can understand how it would feel like morning."

"Coming out of Cryo is no joke," Jenkins adds. She looks toward Michael with a slight smirk. "Robinson here says you took it like a champ, though."

"Well, if we're all finished wagging our chins," LC Hall says, sweeping a gaze over her section, "what do you say we get out there and do our jobs?" Her annoyance is clear on her face.

"Yes ma'am!" The section replies in unison, though with variations of accent. This satisfies the Lance Corporal, and she turns to Aldous.

"Right then! Let's get going. I hope that thing's insulated," she says, gesturing at the jumpsuit, "because it's gonna be a cold one out there."

Aldous does not have time to respond before the starsailor's door opens and lets in a blast of freezing cold air that hits his face like a boxer's punch. It nearly knocks the breath out of him, but he recovers just in time to see that LC Hall has already started out into the cold. She meets a man on the platform, someone wearing the same color orange as the prisoners still inside. As the rest of the section form a perimeter around him, Aldous walks out onto the first non-Earth soil he's ever stepped on.

His foot nearly skids on the icy surface, and he feels only the loosest connection to the ground beneath him. He tries to take another step and feels himself float forward with more speed than he anticipated. Li, from his left side, grabs Aldous by the back of his jumpsuit and brings him back into position between herself and Michael.

"Careful, sir. Less gravity here than our moon." Li's breath clouds out from the hood of her cold-weather uniform.

"Thanks," Aldous says through chattering teeth, "Ah'll bear tha' in mind."

He looks around at the Atmodome, taking in the tinted glass and the warming lamps that orbit it in a mimicry of Earth's sun, an effort to keep the human officials' circadian rhythms as stable as possible while off planet. In spite of the lamps, the cold is still bitter and intense, and Aldous wishes that the jumpsuit had a hood of some kind, or that he had a hat. Still, the parts of him that *are* covered by the jumpsuit are as warm as anyone could reasonably expect them to be thanks to the lining. Aldous blesses his forbears for their plaid invention as he shuffles toward Lance Corporal Hall, who is much farther away from him than he initially thought.

In his slow progress, he sees buildings all around him and in the distance, ranging from military outposts and industrial centers to residential and penitentiary homes. The residence of Fisian Moon 1's Lord Governor stands out to him, opulence epitomized. Brick imported from Earth forms a high wall, with a wrought-iron gate allowing the front of the house to be visible. Imported marble sparkles in the lamp-sunlight as if made from the same ice that makes up the ground outside. The front door, one made of rosewood and carved with intricate scroll designs, opens; a human woman in a muted orange jumpsuit comes out to sweep the shifting ice from the front step. Aldous can see inside now, just for a moment, and looks at the foyer. He sees a sparkling crystal chandelier that casts tiny rainbows all over the black marble floor, the fine art on the walls, and the polished wood of the staircase. Before Aldous could see any more, Lance Corporal Hill grabs his attention.

"Mr. Fairley, this is Liam Caldwel, one of the technicians from the factory where the machine is. He's going to act as a liaison of sorts between you and the machine's creator. Any questions you have, you direct them to him."

Liam looks like the man in Jen's pictures, the husband she lost to transportation ten years ago – fifteen years ago now – and who inspired her work. His tan skin has gone a bit pale because of his distance from the sun, and his hair is streaked with a bit more gray, but the green eyes still sparkle as he smiles, wide and friendly. He reaches out to shake Aldous' hand, gripping it tight. Aldous does the same, relieved to see a somewhat familiar face in all of this.

"Mr. Caldwel, it's good to meechye!"

"Please, call me Liam. Bit quicker, ya know."

"Of course, I understand. Liam, then."

"Well, if you'll follow me, I'll getcha to the human entrance, so 'at you can meet Adthe and startcha studies!" Liam turns with a grace that he has acquired from half a decades' worth of work on this moon. He looks back to see Aldous still shuffling along while he strides forward with confidence. He laughs a little and shakes his head. This guy doesn't seem like the type to harm even a fly. Addie and her mechanical kid have nothing to worry about.

As they walk, Aldous sees more and more of the factory. He sees how it was built into the edge of the Atmodome, allowing the humans to stay fully within the dome and the Hu'Tu and Fisian workers to enter outside, keeping their time in the human atmosphere and temperatures to a minimum. The outside is concrete, gray and drab, with only a sign over the door and smokestacks leading outside the dome to identify it as anything other than a concrete box.

Adthe taps her foot on the floor of the observation booth. Her head rests in her upper right hand, and both of her left hands drum on the desk in front of her. How long does she have to wait for this man to arrive? Why could he not just *get* here and end her suffering, one way or another. She breathes slowly, willing her heart to slow and her temperature to fall. He will arrive when he arrives. She cannot hurry him by wallowing in stress. She sees Supervisor Thoon approach Zhah, one of the young Hu'Tu loaders. The Supervisor leans down and whispers into their ear, and Zhah moves from their station near the Hleh‡de Tisk'Ah. She watches him run across the factory floor, right to the Human entrance. She jumps up from her seat when she sees them try to open the Human door.

The door opens as the group approaches, held open by a young Hu'Tu. They wear the same baggy coveralls and short hairstyles as the other Hu'Tu workers. Aldous stops, and Kapoor nearly runs into him. Aldous doesn't want to, but he stares. In Earth years, this child would be around age seven, so small that they struggle to hold the heavy door. Aldous sees the hair, dark purple and a little shaggy over their pink eyes. Their skin is on the red side of violet. Liam rushes forward.

"Zhah, get back inside! It's too warm out here for you!"

"Gyee'too'kuh Thoon-Vai-"

"I don't care what they said, you get on inside. I've got the door." The Hu'Tu looks unsteady on their feet, but they try to keep hold of the door. One stern look from Liam sends them scrambling inside to the slightly cooler area of the factory, farthest from the Melter, to resume their position. Liam looks back to Aldous and waves his hand in a grand arc, welcoming him inside. Adthe stands inside, watching Zhah run. She turns back to face Liam and sees the army section surrounding a Human she does not know. She looks at Liam, a question on her lips, but turns away before she can ask it, hastening towards her machine. She brushes past Raht and his partner at the Melter, and before her brother can formulate a question, Adthe sends a telepathic message.

"*It is him.*"

Lance Corporal Hall nods to Liam as she steps through the door. Ivarsson does the same, and all the rest follow. Aldous notices the sound, first. He hears the Melter's fire roaring, the scrap metal crashing into its melting place, the whirring of conveyor belts, the hissing of cooling metal. Each sound, on its own, would be enough to overwhelm him on a normal day. Today, hearing all of them at once, all around him, after the sensory hell that he went through earlier, makes him dizzy. He would have fallen to his knees if Michael hadn't grabbed his arm.

"Easy now, sir. Wouldn't want you passing out on us, now would we?"

"Thank you, Mic- er, Private Robinson. I appreciate the assist."

"If you'd like, we've got some ear plugs over in the human lockers," Liam offers. "I'm not sure how much good they'll do ya, but they might at least give ya a bit to adjust."

"Ah'll be fine, thanks. I'd rather jus' go ahead an' get started."

Liam nods and turns his back to Aldous, heading toward the large machine at the other end of the factory line. Before too long, though, he stops and turns back.

"If it's alright with you, Lance Corporal, I think Worker Xi'Adthe would be in a better position to help if she were more comfortable and, no offence, but I don't know of too many who are comfortable when surrounded by British soldiers. Maybe choose one or two of your section to come with us, and let the rest hang back a bit?"

Hall opens her mouth to respond, but Liam interrupts her.

"I know you're here for protection, and I appreciate that, really I do. However, I can personally vouch for the workers in this factory, for their disinterest in any kind of violence or political action. The most you might get is someone who's a bit snippy in the heat of a moment. Stay where you can see Mr. Fairley, by all means, but maybe we treat 'im less like a visiting dignitary and a bit more like a visiting technician."

Aldous looks around. Ivarsson looks to the Lance Corporal, as do all of the other soldiers. From his profile, Aldous can tell that Ivarsson sees no harm in the idea. Li seems more skeptical.

Aldous cannot see Kapoor, and cannot tell what Michael is thinking as his face is turned away and his body language is inscrutable. Kapoor speaks up first.

"I volunteer to stay behind, ma'am," she says, "and keep watch for other threats."

"I will as well," adds Ivarsson.

"I'd be glad to go with Mr. Fairley, ma'am." Michael finally turns his face back toward Aldous, and he winks. "After all, I've been here before, so I don't have much of a desire to look around it again."

Lance Corporal Hall considers for a moment. It *would* be more beneficial to have Kapoor and Ivarsson on watch, since their sight was best, and to have Li and herself with them for backup or covering other avenues of attack. And Robinson seems to have bonded with their charge pretty quickly after Cryo.

"Very well. I agree to your suggestion, Prisoner Caldwel. Robinson, you go with Mr. Fairley. The rest of us will provide support from a distance. Understood?" She looks around at her section.

"Yes ma'am," they all answer in unison. Hall nods, and Liam, Aldous, and Michael continue forward.

As they approach, Aldous can see just how massive the machine is. From the image in his mission briefing, he knew it would be large, but he did not expect it to tower over him, or to be twice as wide as he is. He did not expect the arms to extend out eight feet, by his estimation, and yet to move so fluidly when every other part of it seems so solid and heavy.

Adthe stands beside her creation, the day she has dreaded finally here. She closes her eyes and breathes in deeply, willing her body to freeze like the ice outside. As she does so, her skin loses all of the pink tinges it had moments ago, approaching the blue side of purple. She opens her eyes to see Liam and two other Humans in front of her.

"Xi'Adthe, this is Mr. Aldous Fairley, the roboticist." He indicates the Scotsman to her and she nods, fiddling with the fingers of her lower hands behind her back. "And this is Private Robinson, Mr. Fairley's escort."

Though tense, Adthe manages to keep her body cool and nod to the soldier as well. She meets Liam's eye, and he can see a tinge of a tremble in her stance. He takes a deep breath and winks at her, wishing that he could communicate with her without the others hearing. Hoping she would still receive it even if she couldn't hear his thoughts, he dwells on how confident he is in her, how much he knows she can handle this and that her machine will do amazing things, even if she and it are stuck here. Adthe takes a deep breath.

"Wel'come." Her voice is slow, measured, careful. She wants to make sure she is understood as clearly as possible, though having Liam near helps her feel more at ease. She knows that, if she forgets a word or cannot say it right, he can clarify. "How can I hel' you, mis'ter-"

"Ach, no need for the 'mister,' lass." Aldous speaks before he thinks, wishing after a moment that he hadn't interrupted her. "Jus' Aldous is fine!" He tries to smile, make her feel more comfortable, but she looks more shaken than she did before.

"Right. Al'dous. I will try to re'mem'ber." Adthe regains her composure and continues speaking. "Is there an'y'thing I can tell you be'fore you start your stu'dy?"

She brings her lower hands out from behind her back and lets them hang at her sides. They feel warm, but she cannot cool them without drawing attention to them. She hopes that the airflow will cool them enough.

"Ah'm no' sure, really. Ah'd need to take a preliminary look first, tae see wha' kind of system ye've got runnin'. Bu', if Ah dae end up having questions, ye'll be the first tae know." Aldous turns to look at Liam. "Assumin' tha's arigh' with Liam, here, seein' as how he's meant to get mah questions."

"Works just fine with me! Honestly, you'd be better hearing from the source anyway, since I don't know shit about how this thing runs!" He smiles at Adthe. "This one's too smart for me, honestly." Adthe blushes despite her efforts to remain cold and unreadable. A sharp tone comes from the PA speakers, followed by a rough voice.

"Mr. Fairley, Worker Xi'Adthe, Worker Caldwel, report to the Control Office immediately."

Adthe and Liam look up, and Aldous follows their gaze to a bank of windows that stretch across half of the wall beside them. In one window is a figure with four arms, all crossed over their chest, and slicked-back hair. All Aldous could tell beyond that was a vague purple color to the figure, but he was unsure if it was the clothing or the person themselves who bore the color. Adthe and Liam caught each other's eye. What does Vai want now? Liam turns to Aldous.

"That's our Supervisor, Thoon-Vai. Our next step was to introduce you to 'em anyway, since they're the one who'll handle your report and all that. If you'll follow me and Adthe, we'll head on up there now." Liam leads the way, followed by Aldous and Michael.

Adthe stays to the back of the line, wringing both sets of hands. Her thoughts begin to spiral again. What could Vai want so urgently? Are they just upset that the roboticist met her first instead of heading straight into the Control Office? Adthe's heart beats harder with every step on the staircase. It takes more and more effort to keep her breathing and body temperature steady.

When the door opens for Liam, he continues moving. His thoughts are with Adthe, hoping that she's feeling alright. He knows how much she'd hoped to avoid this day somehow. This wrinkle has to be kicking her into emotional overdrive. A guard stops Michael before he can enter the room.

"Not you," the man says in a gruff voice. "He'll be safe enough in here with all of us." Michael looks to Aldous to gauge how he should proceed. Aldous nods.

"Don' worry. Ah'm sure it'll be fine!" He gives what he hopes is a reassuring smile as Michael steps aside to let Adthe pass him. As the door closes, Aldous sees that Michael waits right outside the door, in the "at ease" position.

"Welcome, Mr. Fairley, to Fisian Moon 1 and to our facility. I am Thoon-Vai, and I am the Factory Supervisor." They extend their top right hand toward Aldous. They have to reach down because of their height, standing at least a head taller than Aldous.

Something about Vai reminds him of Chief Constable Edwards. Maybe the eyes? He shakes away the thought and accepts their handshake. They grip tight, tighter than Liam had, and hold on for just a little too long. The silence is tense, as no one speaks and no noise penetrates the room apart from the very muffled sound of the factory's work below.

Adthe shifts her weight from foot to foot, wringing both sets of hands behind her back. Aldous grimaces as the grip on his hand tightens even more. Liam stares down Vai, daring in the face of the Supervisor's attempt to establish some kind of dominance. Finally, they release Aldous' hand.

"Well!" Aldous says, rubbing the hand that Vai had nearly crushed. "Tha's quite a grip!"

"I will take that as complimentary. Now, to the business at hand. Mr. Fairley, what are your mission parameters?" Vai shoots a glance at Adthe. She freezes in place.

"Um, shouldnae ye know my mission already? Given 'at I'm supposed to report tae ye and all-"

"I am aware of your mission parameters, yes. Still," they lean in close to Aldous' face, "indulge me." Liam is fuming. Adthe is still frozen in her place. Aldous leans away from Vai and clears his throat.

"Well, ah, my mission is tae find out what makes the Hlehdeh Tisk'Ah work so efficiently so that other facilities can replicate it for their own inspection needs."

Vai smirks, and Adthe cringes, at the mispronunciation of the machine's name. Aldous doesn't notice, too wrapped up in the questions shooting from one end of his brain to the other. Where is this going? Why were they asking this? The two questions go back and forth like the ball in a championship tennis match.

"Study in order to replicate. Is there anything that you could think of that would hinder that mission?" Vai's eyes stay on Adthe, and the woman begins to shuffle her feet again.

"Ah'm no' sure I understand the question." Aldous also looks to Adthe and Vai, struggling to understand any of what was happening. He looks to Liam and sees the anger in his eyes. He looks back to Vai. "I feel like I'm missing sommat here-"

"Perhaps the question *was* unclear," Vai interrupts, their voice snide and condescending. "Let me rephrase: Is there anything, say, for instance, a change in the machine's behavior, that would make your mission difficult or change it entirely?"

"I, ah, I suppose it would depend on the nature of the change?" Aldous continues to look at the people around him, human, Fisian, and Hu'Tu, trying to get some idea of how this situation was supposed to unfold, if anyone else is as lost as he is.

Liam is still fuming, balling his hands into fists and restraining himself from speaking. He knows that nothing he could say would make the situation any better, and would likely only make things worse for Adthe in the long run. He would rather comfort her later than make the situation worse in ways he can't see coming.

Adthe is shaking now; her skin is flushed a deep red, and her face betrays all of the dread and fear that she had been trying to hide for the whole conversation. Vai knows. They know about her miracle, about her *baby*. They know about the differences, the quirks, they've *noticed* all of it. She wants nothing more than to run, to rip the core out of the machine and just flee to a place where no one would know her, where no one will find her, where she and her miracle can be safe. Her breaths come shallow, rapid, and uneven. She wants to run, but she is frozen in place, trembling violently. She cannot leave until Vai dismisses her.

Vai is triumphant. If this does not lead to the destruction of that family, then they have misread every situation leading to this one. A father, accused of sedition and high treason; a mother, dead from heartbreak; a brother, wishing for an opportunity to execute his father's dangerous ideas; and a sister who wanted nothing more than to help her brother and his fellow workers, brought down by the very thing that she created. It is just too perfect. Vai glories in the feeling.

Aldous' mind is reeling. He's putting together the pieces, fitting together an advanced inspection system with a reported ability to learn from prior inspections. Adding in the mention of quirks in behavior that have appeared in the time since he was dispatched from Earth. Reading Adthe's terror, Liam's anger, and Vai's smugness, and adding them into the mix. One explanation comes to mind. One impossible and alluring explanation that he almost hopes to be true. This miracle, this machine that Adthe built, is *alive*.

"Mr. Fairley, I am adjusting your mission parameters." Vai's sharp voice cuts through Aldous' revelations. He looks at them and nods, indicating that he is listening. "If the aforementioned behavioral changes do not impact the machine's efficiency, then by all means, study it for reproduction elsewhere. I would be *overjoyed* to see technology pioneered at my facility benefit the empires at large." Their lip curls, betraying their sarcasm. "*If*, however, there is something impeding the machine in its duties, then I expect you to find it, report it, and advise on how to eradicate it. The scale could be as small as deleting a line of code, or as large as destroying the machine entirely. That is at your discretion. Do you understand your new parameters?"

"Aye." Aldous looks at Adthe and Liam, hoping they catch his meaning. "I understand the new parameters."

www.ingramcontent.com/pod-product-compliance
Lightning Source LLC
LaVergne TN
LVHW020955200726
843506LV00012B/2127